Critical Thinking

Make strategic decisions with confidence

Second Edition

Daniel A. Feldman, Ph.D.

A Crisp Fifty-Minute™ Series Book

AXZO PRESS

Critical Thinking

Make strategic decisions with confidence

Second Edition

Daniel A. Feldman, Ph.D.

CREDITS:

President, Axzo Press:	**Jon Winder**
Vice President, Product Development:	**Charles G. Blum**
Vice President, Operations:	**Josh Pincus**
Director, Publishing Systems Development:	**Dan Quackenbush**
Copy Editor:	**Catherine M. Albano**

Trademarks

Crisp Fifty-Minute Series is a trademark of Axzo Press.

Some of the product names and company names used in this book have been used for identification purposes only and may be trademarks or registered trademarks of their respective manufacturers and sellers.

Disclaimer

We reserve the right to revise this publication and make changes from time to time in its content without notice.

ISBN 10: 1-4260-1853-3
ISBN 13: 978-1-4260-1853-4
Printed in the United States of America
1 2 3 4 5 11 10 09

Table of Contents

Appendix 89

About the Author

Daniel Feldman is owner and president of Leadership Performance Solutions, Inc., an organizational development consulting company. Daniel provides a variety of senior level coaching and consulting services, including: leadership development, process facilitation, organizational review, team development, strategic and action planning, organizational design and restructuring, conflict resolution, process improvement, and change management. Daniel regularly coaches senior staff and facilitates senior level meetings and retreats.

Daniel has provided comprehensive executive coaching and facilitation services in the private sector for large and small companies in a variety of industries, including technology, healthcare, financial services, and hospitality and has delivered organization-wide transformation interventions to federal agencies.

Daniel has designed, developed, and delivered a wide-range of human capital development training programs and is a Certified Professional Facilitator by the International Association of Facilitators. He is the author of *The Handbook of Emotionally Intelligent Leadership* and *The Manager's Pocket Guide to Workplace Coaching*. Daniel received his M.S. and Ph.D. degrees in Counseling Psychology from Virginia Commonwealth University and is a licensed psychologist.

For information about programs and presentations based on this book, contact:

Leadership Performance Solutions, Inc.
Paonia, Colorado
800.511.6150
dafeldman@leadershipperformance.com

Preface

This book offers step-by-step guidance for strengthening the thinking skills necessary to grapple with the deluge of information we face daily, particularly at work. How can you determine the validity of an argument given by a co-worker? How can you explain the underlying cause of a shift in customer demand or the importance of a work process?

This book contains three parts. Part 1 introduces critical thinking and presents the pitfalls of non-critical thinking tactics. It explores the differences between ineffective and effective thinking styles and gives overall strategies for developing critical thinking.

Part 2 focuses on recognizing and evaluating arguments. It teaches the importance of recognizing the elements of an argument and the methods for judging the validity of an argument. It also gives direction for presenting effective arguments.

Part 3 enumerates steps for developing and evaluating explanations. It describes how to gather and process information and develop and test hypotheses. It also describes common errors in information processing.

Do you want to learn overall strategies for improving your critical thinking skills? If so, practice the exercises in Part 1.

Are people trying to convince you to adopt their point of view? If so, use the steps in Part 2 for recognizing and evaluating arguments.

Do you want to understand and explain a situation? If so, follow the steps in Part 3 for developing and evaluating explanations.

Together, the three parts of this book offer valuable guidance on how to make effective decisions in the workplace.

Daniel Feldman, Ph.D.

Acknowledgments

Much appreciation to Jeff Kelly for his insights and assistance. Enduring thanks to all my family—in particular my wife, Jo—for their tremendous support and encouragement. Heartfelt gratitude to Gurumayi Chidvilasananda for her continual loving guidance.

Learning Objectives

Complete this book, and you'll know how to:

1) Explain the differences between critical and noncritical thinking.

2) Improve the thinking necessary to make effective decisions at work.

3) Evaluate the validity of arguments.

4) Use evidence to support strong arguments and explanations.

5) Formulate effective explanations with solid information and reasoned hypotheses.

Workplace and Management Competencies mapping

For over 30 years, business and industry has utilized competency models to select employees. The trend to use competency-based approaches in education and training, assessment, and development of workers has experienced a more recent emergence within the Employment and Training Administration (ETA), a division of the United States Department of Labor.

The ETA's General Competency Model Framework spans a wide array of competencies from the more basic competencies, such as reading and writing, to more advanced occupation-specific competencies. The Crisp Series finds its home in what the ETA refers to as the Workplace Competencies and the Management Competencies.

Critical Thinking covers information vital to mastering the following competencies:

Workplace Competencies:

▶ Creative Thinking

Management Competencies:

▶ Managing Conflict & Team Building

For a comprehensive mapping of Crisp Series titles to the Workplace and Management competencies, visit www.CrispSeries.com.

About the Crisp 50-Minute Series

The Crisp 50-Minute Series was designed to cover critical business and professional development topics in the shortest possible time. Our easy-to-read, easy-to-understand format can be used for self-study or for classroom training. With a wealth of hands-on exercises, the 50-Minute books keep you engaged and help you retain critical skills.

What You Need to Know

We designed the Crisp 50-Minute Series to be as self-explanatory as possible. But there are a few things you should know before you begin the book.

Exercises

Exercises look like this:

EXERCISE TITLE

Questions and other information would be here.

Keep a pencil handy. Any time you see an exercise, you should try to complete it. If the exercise has specific answers, an answer key will be provided in the appendix. (Some exercises ask you to think about your own opinions or situation; these types of exercises will not have answer keys.)

Forms

A heading like this means that the rest of the page is a form:

FORMHEAD

Forms are meant to be reusable. You might want to make a photocopy of a form before you fill it out, so that you can use it again later.

A Note to Instructors

We've tried to make the Crisp 50-Minute Series books as useful as possible as classroom training manuals. Here are some of the features we provide for instructors:

- ▶ PowerPoint presentations
- ▶ Answer keys
- ▶ Assessments
- ▶ Customization

PowerPoint Presentations

You can download a PowerPoint presentation for this book from our Web site at www.CrispSeries.com.

Answer keys

If an exercise has specific answers, an answer key will be provided in the appendix. (Some exercises ask you to think about your own opinions or situation; these types of exercises will not have answer keys.)

Assessments

For each 50-Minute Series book, we have developed a 35- to 50-item assessment. The assessment for this book is available at www.CrispSeries.com. *Assessments should not be used in any employee-selection process.*

Customization

Crisp books can be quickly and easily customized to meet your needs—from adding your logo to developing proprietary content. Crisp books are available in print and electronic form. For more information on customization, see www.CrispSeries.com.

P A R T 1

Understanding Critical vs. Noncritical Thinking

In this part:

- ▶ The Case for Critical Thinking
- ▶ Recognize Deceptive Reasoning
- ▶ Detect Emotional Manipulation
- ▶ Styles of Noncritical Thinking
- ▶ Critical Thinking Styles
- ▶ Become a Critical Thinker

The Case for Critical Thinking

We live and work in a world of ever-accelerating change, where information multiplies exponentially and job requirements constantly shift. More than ever, we must be able to reasonably challenge "standard operating procedure" or workflow processes. Faced with frequent choices about strategy and direction, employees today need the skills of critical thinking to choose the most effective path.

Decision-Making at Work

At work, we make decisions based on the information available to us. For example, imagine that Bob approaches you and says in a very serious tone:

> *"If you put that conclusion in the report, you'll be looking for a new job by Monday! The boss never likes new ideas. Look what happened to Chris. He's out on the street now."*

How should you respond to this statement? How much weight should you give it in deciding what to put in the report? Should you accept Bob's comments at face value and change what you wrote? Should you ignore it? What should you believe?

While trying to decide the correct path, we often develop explanations and evaluate statements that may or may not be true, or that may be true but not relevant. Co-workers try to persuade us to adopt a point of view, and we present our ideas and opinions to persuade them. We also generate a host of ideas and statements within our own minds:

> *"We should form an action team for this initiative."*

> *"I think it would be best to focus on the needs assessment rather than the financial report."*

> *"I think the finance department is unappreciated because no one sees their work."*

How can we successfully evaluate all this information to make effective decisions at work? We'll use the power of critical thinking.

Benefits of Critical Thinking

Critical thinking involves evaluating a situation, problem, or argument and choosing a path of investigation that leads to the best possible answers. Listed below are benefits of critical thinking at work. Check the three that you would most like to bring to your job.

- ❑ Recognize your own biases to guide self-improvement.

- ❑ Contribute to teams through what you say and do.

- ❑ Gain the respect of both your manager and your co-workers.

- ❑ Develop the best solutions to problems.

- ❑ Gain greater insight into the motives of others.

- ❑ Give sound arguments to create buy-in for your ideas.

- ❑ Identify key issues without getting sidetracked.

- ❑ Write and speak with impact.

- ❑ Improve customer service through greater understanding of customer needs.

This book will provide you with a set of guidelines and skills for critical thinking. But first, let's look at the alternative and see what can happen when *non*critical thinking is used.

"You should only believe half of what you read.
The trick is deciding which half."

THE PITFALLS OF NONCRITICAL THINKING

Below is a list of pitfalls that can occur from noncritical thinking. Check those that you or your colleagues have fallen into in the past month. For each one identified, write what happened and the consequences.

For example, under "stupid mistakes" you might write:

What happened: *HR failed to tell staff about the changes in leave policy.*

Consequences: *All the timesheets had to be redone.*

❑ **Stupid mistakes**

What happened: _____

Consequences: _____

❑ **Promoting a dud of an idea**

What happened: _____

Consequences: _____

❑ **Wrong decisions**

What happened: _____

Consequences: _____

❑ **Disputes and disagreements because of misinformation**

What happened: _____

Consequences: _____

❑ **Wasted time from being sidetracked**

What happened: _____

Consequences: _____

❑ **Believing there was buy-in when there was not**

What happened: _____

Consequences: _____

Most of these pitfalls were probably due to noncritical thinking. Next we'll explore noncritical thinking tactics used to influence others, to avoid unwittingly agreeing to something that isn't based on sound reasoning.

Recognize Deceptive Reasoning

We practice critical thinking when we carefully and deliberately use reasoning strategies to reach a decision about what to believe or do. When people operate in noncritical styles, they slip into errors in reasoning. Deceptive reasoning tactics distort the reasoning process. The tactics might be intentional or unintentional.

Deceptive reasoning techniques include:

- ▶ Using irrelevant facts
- ▶ Avoiding uncomfortable facts
- ▶ Oversimplifying
- ▶ Arguing from ignorance
- ▶ Appealing to the multitude
- ▶ Presenting a false cause
- ▶ Begging the question
- ▶ Attacking the person
- ▶ Creating a "straw man"
- ▶ Sliding down a slippery slope

Using Irrelevant Facts

Definition: Citing facts that don't apply to the matter at hand.

Example: *"We're going to have a new company president in the next few months, so we might as well take it easy until he is selected."*

How to handle irrelevant facts: Point out the irrelevance of the fact.

> *"Yes, we are getting a new president, but I think that is irrelevant to the level of effort we put into the job."*

Avoiding Uncomfortable Facts

Definition: Omitting facts that do not support your argument.

Example: *"Ineffective marketing has caused a drop in the demand for our product, so we are reducing the marketing department staff by 20%."*

How to handle avoiding uncomfortable facts: Point out the missing fact.

> *"Financial reports show there has been a major slowdown in the economy. I wonder if this is one factor you haven't considered."*

Oversimplifying

Definition: Making something sound less complex to the point of error.

Example: *"The increase in workload, the hiring freeze, and the reduction in benefits happened because the senior staff likes to shake things up."*

How to handle oversimplifying: Point out the illogic and mention other evidence that suggests a more complicated argument.

> *"I'm not sure that would be the only reason for the senior staff to make all those changes. I suspect major changes in company policy are influenced by many factors."*

Arguing from Ignorance

Definition: Taking a position based on the fact that it has never been disproved.

Example: *"I've never seen a more efficient way to go about it, so I guess this workflow process is the best there is."*

How to handle arguing from ignorance: Explain the limitations this has for proving a point.

> *"I understand you haven't seen a better way. But if we ever want to improve something, it takes research and looking at new ideas."*

Appealing to the Multitude

Definition: Seeking agreement because the idea is supported by many people.

Example: *"We should use X brand printer paper because most people use it."*

How to handle appealing to the multitude: Mention the lack of support the statement has for the conclusion.

> *"That's like saying '50 million people can't be wrong.' Well, sometimes they can be. X brand paper may be popular, but that has nothing to do with the unique specifications and requirements of our printers."*

Presenting a False Cause

Definition: Claiming that one event causes another simply because it happens at around the same time.

Example: Valentina is friendly and outgoing. Jonathan is more introverted and quiet. Shortly after they are moved into a new workspace, Jonathan becomes less productive at work. Jonathan's supervisor says, *"Jonathan's work is suffering because Valentina talks too much."*

This is a false cause because no corroborating facts link the move to Jonathan's decreased efficiency. It could be due to his having a hard time changing in general or getting a new task that he does not know how to handle. Perhaps he has personal difficulties that happened to start about the same time as the move.

How to handle presenting a false cause: Point out the lack of connection that exists in the statement.

> *"Moving in with Valentina may have affected Jonathan's work, but so far there has been no proof there is any relationship between her talkativeness and his effectiveness."*

Begging the Question

Definition: Making a claim that is supported only by itself. This is also known as circular reasoning.

Example: *"You be the note taker and I'll be the leader for the meeting."*
"Why should you be the leader for the meeting?"
"Because you'll be taking the notes!"

How to handle begging the question: Challenge the reasoning and ask for a more convincing piece of evidence.

> *"Let's start from the beginning without either of us having an assigned role. Now, I'd like to discuss the criteria we want for a leader for this meeting."*

Attacking the Person

Definition: Falsely discounting an argument by discrediting the person making it.

Example: *"Janet says she has found a flaw in the financial analysis. I don't trust her judgment because Janet doesn't have a college degree."*

How to handle attacking the person: Point out the irrelevance these attacks have to the argument.

> *"Janet's not having a degree isn't relevant to this particular piece of work. Let's focus on the reasons she gives for the mistake."*

Creating a "Straw Man"

Definition: Distorting the conclusion of another and then attacking that misrepresented position.

Example:

Josh: *"I think we should not keep working into the evening because we are more alert during the day."*

Kathy: *"Josh is suggesting we don't have the character to handle the extra work load. Personally, I resent this attack on my dedication. I think we are an extremely committed group and should keep working into the night."*

How to handle creating a "straw man": Refocus on the original position.

Josh: *"I also think we are a committed group. But my point had nothing to do with character or commitment and everything to do with effectiveness."*

Sliding Down a Slippery Slope

Definition: Arguing against a conclusion by implying it is linked to another conclusion even though the link between the two is tenuous or weak.

Example: *"If we give employees flex time, they will expect more and more benefits and eventually we'll be giving them a four-day workweek!"*

How to handle sliding down a slippery slope: Examine each conclusion one at a time.

"Giving employees flex time may or may not lead them to expect more benefits. If they do expect more benefits, this may or may not lead them to ask for a four-day workweek. Let's look at each of these points one at a time."

Detect Emotional Manipulation

We all come across emotional manipulations regularly. Techniques that fall into this category attempt to sway others primarily through emotions. Being aware of these techniques arms us against being manipulated. But using emotionally manipulative tactics does not automatically invalidate the case being presented. Pick and choose what makes sense.

Emotional manipulation techniques include:

▶ Inflammatory words

▶ Pressure tactics

▶ Appeals to sentiment

▶ Ridicule

Inflammatory Words

Definition: Arousing or expressing feelings of approval or disapproval to get others to concede. Inflammatory words evoke emotions that may be untrue or irrelevant to the situation under review.

Example: *"He's a 'B' player."*
"That's a radioactive assignment."
"She's a clock watcher."

How to handle inflammatory words: Rephrase them into more neutral words, forcing the speaker to consider and clarify the message she is conveying. This helps you both to determine if the statement is relevant or accurate. For example:

Following *"He's a 'B' player,"* you could say, *"Do you mean he has been less productive than his co-workers?"*

To *"That's a radioactive assignment,"* you could respond, *"Do you mean it is a difficult and politically sensitive assignment?"*

After *"She's a clock watcher,"* you could ask, *"Do you mean she works the minimum amount of time required?"*

Pressure Tactics

Definition: Intimidating others into agreement.

Example: *"You'll make your boss unhappy."*
"The whole office will see you as a pariah."

How to handle pressure tactics: Ignore them. If this does not work, restate such statements in a neutral manner and ask for clarification. For example:

To *"You'll make your boss unhappy,"* you might respond, *"In what way will the boss be unhappy?"*

After *"The whole office will see you as a pariah,"* you could ask, *"Whom do you mean by 'the whole office' and what will they not like?"*

Appeals to Sentiment

Definition: Using pity or compassion to get others to accept particular conclusions.

Example: *"Bob should get a promotion because he has eight kids."*

How to handle appeals to sentiment: Shift the conversation back to the argument at hand. For example, in responding to *"Bob should get a promotion because he has eight kids,"* you might say, *"I realize Bob has a large family. But is he the best person for the job?"*

Ridicule

Definition: Saying something to make others appear contemptible as a way of forcing them to concede to a position.

Example: *"Why do you want to appear ignorant by not agreeing with rest of us?"*

How to handle ridicule: Point out the ridicule and question it. For example, in response to *"Why do you want to appear ignorant by not agreeing with everyone else?"* You might say, *"'Appearing ignorant' is a strong accusation. What do you mean by that?"*

Tip: *Emotional manipulation in and of itself may provide important information about a situation. It just doesn't provide evidence in support of the conclusion of the argument.*

EXERCISE: THE MANIPULATIVE MEMO

Meg wrote the memo that follows. She is a consultant working on a project for a large government agency. She wrote the memo to Allen, a consultant from a different consulting company, who is working on the same project.

Read the following memo. Circle and label any emotional manipulation tactics you detect.

Dear Allen,

I am writing this memo because I am concerned about the explosive e-mail you sent last week and hope you will send out a retraction of some of your key points.

Based on what you wrote, I thought you overreached your authority. I believe that if I went to the senior project manager about this, he would agree with me. This would seriously impair the ability of your company to participate in other projects at this agency.

The fact that you sent the e-mail to all of the project participants supports the impression that you have only a rudimentary understanding of the appropriate channels of communication.

Meg

Rewrite the memo in a more neutral tone, without using emotional manipulation tactics.

_____

_____

_____

_____

_____

_____

_____

_____

EXERCISE: EXAMINING THE EMOTION

Write a statement someone made to you this week that included an emotional manipulation tactic, such as "I'm sick and tired of upper management moving us around like pawns."

_____

_____

_____

Ask yourself: What is the emotional impact of the specific words used in this statement?

_____

_____

_____

_____

_____

Styles of Noncritical Thinking

As you have learned, *non*critical thinking is black and white, dogmatic, and uninformed. It is passive, shallow, and reactive. Noncritical thinking operates from a narrow and limiting frame of reference, with continual pressure to doubt or exclude new ideas or ways of doing things.

A common feature of noncritical thinking is a refusal to evaluate objectively our own thought process, which shows up in several ways:

▶ "Closed-minded" thinking, which involves rigidly adhering to a previous point of view regardless of new evidence presented

▶ Excessive receptivity to every new idea presented in the mistaken belief that all opinions are equally valid

▶ Lazy thinking, which is a failure to analyze ideas fully

The various forms of noncritical thinking can be grouped in particular styles. Anyone can fall into any of the noncritical ways of thinking some of the time. We might fall into a particular style depending on the circumstances, such as being in a planning session with the manager or dealing with an unfamiliar situation. Some people, however, operate in one of these styles most of the time.

Tip: *It is OK to make imperfect decisions sometimes. Remind yourself that developing critical thinking skills is an ongoing process. The only real mistake is failing to learn from your imperfect decisions.*

Style	Traits
The Grinch	Closed-minded Suspicious Overly stubborn Rigid
The Dilettante	Overly receptive Vague Resents discipline Distractible
The Snob	Self-deluded Arrogant Excessively confident in his own conclusion Egotistical
The Emoter*	Vacillates between beliefs according to changing mood Reacts purely emotionally Does not look at underlying assumptions Makes excuses Does not examine the details of an argument
The Leech	Latches onto whatever someone else thinks Accepts information uncritically Avoids difficult problems Is lazy Is passive and dependent

---

This is not to say that emotions are not useful. When employed appropriately, they are part of the critical thinking process.

NONCRITICAL STYLES IN ACTION

In the spaces provided, identify the noncritical thinking styles demonstrated by the following stories and write how you determined that style.

1. Zack is a computer programmer. He has an opinion about everything and will comment on anything under discussion. His co-worker Juanita is a Web site developer. When asked if he thinks Juanita could handle a sophisticated assignment, Zack says,

   "How could she? She's only a Web developer. Everybody knows they aren't real techies."

   Zack's noncritical thinking style(s)

   _____

   _____

2. Holly to Arjun:

   "I agree with your plan for the Ballard project. It sounds great."

   Later, after talking about it with another co-worker, Simon, she says to Arjun,

   "I have grave concerns about the Ballard project. Simon doesn't believe it will fly."

   Holly's noncritical thinking style(s)

   _____

   _____

3. Talking to the director of human resources, the senior executive says,

   "I respect your many years of experience and the report from the experts. However, I still think we should ask the opinion of everyone in the office before we decide on how to structure the new pay schedule so everybody can be happy."

   The senior executive's noncritical thinking style(s)

   _____

   _____

Compare your responses to those of the author in the Appendix.

Critical Thinking Styles

Critical thinkers generally are open and recognize many shades of gray. They understand and use the skills of critical thinking to consider different frames of reference and operate with a continual push to find new ideas and options. But there are different individual styles of critical thinking, just as there are for noncritical thinking.

We can use more than one critical thinking style at a time. In fact, the more styles we use together, the better our critical thinking. These styles lead to a deeper understanding of the situation.

Style	Traits
The Explorer	Looks at all sides of a situation or problem Identifies the core element of a problem or situation Is curious Seeks new developments
The Student	Is diligent Researches alternative solutions to problems Does homework Corrects errors
The Warrior	Accepts challenges Perseveres Faces difficult problems
The Navigator	Guides others Looks ahead Plans a course of action
The Detective	Questions own thoughts and actions Tolerates ambiguity Pursues the elusive element of fact

CRITICAL THINKING STYLE FILE

Which critical thinking styles are demonstrated by the following stories? Remember that a person can be demonstrating more than one critical thinking style at a time.

1. The project management team is under pressure from top management to speed up its work. At the next team meeting, the team leader says,

   "We should skip our usual action planning and just come up with some estimates for these jobs."

   Alexa, a team member, interjects,

   "I don't agree. If we do that, we could end up with disastrous results and waste more time. I suggest that we look at how we can speed up our meeting format without sacrificing important steps in our decision-making."

   Alexa's critical thinking style(s)

   _____

   _____

2. Pascal says,

   "I don't think we should automatically go along with the consultant's recommendations. We should ask more questions about how they came up with these results and what the consequences will be if we do or do not implement these changes. I'd be willing to meet with them and discuss all the details of how they came up with these suggestions."

   Pascal's critical thinking style(s)

   _____

   _____

CONTINUED

3. Chandrika says to her manager, Steven,

"I can't format the regulations until George gets me his part of the job. He's always late and it is very frustrating. I think he's just unmotivated and lazy."

Steven answers,

"Before we jump to conclusions, let's find out if there are other reasons why George is late. Perhaps there are factors we don't know about. I wonder what his perspective is. I'd like to talk to George and get more information about what might be going on."

Steven's critical thinking style(s)

_____

_____

4. On Hans' first day on the job, his new manager says,

"I know we hired you as a claims adjuster, but our budget analyst just quit and we need you to help out in this area as well. It will give you a new experience and be of great benefit to the company. We think you can handle it. What about it?"

After contemplating this idea for an hour, Hans goes to see his manager and says,

"Although I am excited about the claims adjuster work, I also would like to try taking on the additional responsibilities. I can't tell you for sure if I will be able to handle both jobs, even on a temporary basis, but I would like to see how it goes. Let's check in a week to see how it goes doing both, and maybe I'll have a clearer perspective about how it might work out long term."

Hans' critical thinking style(s)

_____

_____

Compare your responses to those of the author in the Appendix.

WHAT'S YOUR THINKING STYLE?

Taking another look at the noncritical and critical thinking styles, think about which styles you use most frequently.

Noncritical	Critical
The Grinch	The Explorer
The Dilettante	The Student
The Snob	The Warrior
The Emoter	The Navigator
The Leech	The Detective

The noncritical thinking style I use most frequently is:

_____

_____

The critical thinking style I use most frequently is:

_____

_____

In the next section, you will learn four strategies to help you expand your critical thinking styles and go beyond your noncritical thinking tendencies.

Become a Critical Thinker

It is one thing to understand the benefits of critical thinking, but quite another to put critical thinking to work. When making decisions, apply these four strategies to help you increase your critical thinking:

Strategy 1: *A willingness to look at yourself*

Strategy 2: *Persistent evaluation*

Strategy 3: *Ongoing fair-mindedness*

Strategy 4: *Commitment to an informed decision*

Each of these strategies involves a series of steps, but you cannot devise an exact formula for every decision you must make. Just remember, when you are thinking critically, you should run through these steps. With effort and practice, this approach to critical thinking will become automatic.

Strategy 1: A Willingness to Look at Yourself

As much as possible, practice honest self-awareness and reflection. You can improve your thinking and learning by looking at how you are thinking. You can challenge limiting, habitual styles of thinking and find new ways to look at each situation.

To begin the process of critical thinking, you must first look at your thoughts. Focusing on your thinking can take effort and sometimes can be uncomfortable. When faced with a workplace challenge, you can decide to focus just on the easier parts of the task you are familiar with or you can focus on what you need to learn to succeed. You can respond to a problem in the same old way, or you can look at the patterns of how you think about the problem and discover a newer, improved strategy for dealing with it.

Steps for this strategy:

1. **Ask *why* questions.**

    Instead of accepting things at face value, keep asking why you believe or view things as you do.

2. **Identify and challenge your biases.**

    Biases and stereotypes encourage inaccuracies in perception. Holding onto them is a way to avoid using your "thinking muscles." Once you have identified your biases, exercise your "thinking muscles" as you go through the reasoning steps presented later in this book.

3. **Recognize your thinking process, get rid of unproductive thinking strategies, and learn effective new ones.**

    People use different strategies for how they approach new information, problems, and challenges. Parts 2 and 3 of this book provide approaches that may give you new ideas for your thinking strategies.

Activities:

1. Keep a journal. It does not have to be a chronological diary. Use it as a place to have a conversation with yourself.

2. Schedule 30 minutes a week to review decisions over the past week in which you failed to use critical thinking. Practice the steps for evaluating arguments and explanations with each decision.

3. Look at yourself in the mirror (literally!). Ask yourself:

   What decisions have I made recently in a rushed or superficial way?

   _____

   What do I need to face today that I did not face yesterday? _____

   _____

   How have my biases affected my decisions? _____

   _____

4. Look for your stereotypes. Identify a generalization you hold about work that may be a limiting stereotype (for example, people on the administrative side of the business are not as important as those in the service side).

   _____

   _____

   Is this generalization absolutely true? _____

   _____

   How has this idea affected how I act at work? _____

   _____

   _____

   What would change if I held a different belief? _____

   _____

   _____

Strategy 2: Persistent Evaluation

Learn to actively examine and assess information. Use intellectual courage and perseverance to assess each step of dealing with an issue and to redirect your thinking as you go along.

Be clear about the criteria you are using to evaluate information. Check to see if it is comprehensive and relevant.

Steps for this strategy:

1. **Solicit feedback from other sources.**

   You limit yourself when you evaluate events only from your own perspective. Regularly check documents or solicit perspectives from customers and co-workers.

2. **Appraise the quality of possible answers.**

   Questions have answers that can be deemed either factually right or wrong (facts) or better or worse (opinions). Try to discover the best method for reaching correct or better answers.

3. **Compare your initial goals with your results.**

   By touching base with your goals, you ensure your evaluation stays in line with what you want to accomplish.

Activities:

1. Ask trusted peers for their honest assessment about the progress of your most important current project.

2. Select an ongoing project at work to analyze.

   Ask yourself:

   How can I discriminate between what I really need to focus on to get the job done and what is not really relevant or essential?

   _____

   _____

   _____

3. The next time you are dealing with an issue at work, ask yourself: What is the closest example of this type of problem I have dealt with before? How did I deal with it that time?

   _____

   _____

   _____

4. Identify an area of vulnerability. Are you sensitive to criticism? Do you feel that you lean on your manager too much?

   Now ask yourself:

   How does this hinder my critical thinking?

   How can I get rid of this vulnerability?

   _____

   _____

   _____

Strategy 3: Ongoing Fair-Mindedness

Approach differing opinions with a respectful and open mind. Appreciate not only that many others have a different and useful perspective, but also that your own perspective may be limited or incorrect.

Steps for this strategy:

1. **Accept that others may have a different worldview.**

   Imagine another person's world and upbringing—the values he was taught and the challenges he has faced. Put yourself in his shoes and then view the current situation from his perspective.

2. **Look for points of agreement.**

   When you are having an argument or disagreement, focus on aspects of the opposing points that you could agree with.

3. **Recognize there are often several solutions to a problem.**

   Never stop at your first solution. Approach every problem as if it is an assignment from a client who wants at least three solutions to choose from.

Activities:

1. Think of the colleagues or subordinates for whom you have the least respect. Schedule a time to meet with them and find what you can do to help them be more effective at their job. Learn what you can about their background and values, and try to walk in their shoes.

2. Identify a workplace controversy. Determine the different sides in the controversy. Write an argument for each side. Identify points of agreement.

3. Think of a solution you came up with in the past week. Develop three alternative solutions to the problem that use procedures not usually in your repertoire.

Strategy 4: Commitment to an Informed Decision

Research every important decision you will make as if you will be cross-examined by an expert in that field before a jury of your peers. Try to integrate all available information into your decision.

After everything is said and done, be willing to take a stand.

Steps for this strategy:

1. **Create a clear line of reasoning.**

   Start from your basic assumptions, and build a logical step-by-step progression to the reasonable solution. Challenge each step in the final progression.

2. **Go for the most probable answer rather than waiting for total accuracy.**

   There are too many unknowns in the world to be 100% sure of most things. When you have tested a hypothesis enough to have the courage of your convictions, go with it—while recognizing that it could be improved upon.

3. **Recognize the need for trade-off or consensus in making your decision.**

   In other words, take the decision's social context into account. Remember that your decision must be implemented in the real world, and not an idealized "virtual" world.

Activities:

1. Clearly spell out your reasons for some action you took at work this week.

   Action taken:

   _____

   Reasons:

   _____

   _____

   Identify ways you could have gathered more information before taking this action.

   _____

   _____

2. List three decisions you currently need to make at work for which there is no absolute right or wrong answer.

_____

_____

_____

Analyze the most important one according to the three steps for committing to an informed decision.

Decision: _____

Trace your clear line of reasoning toward that decision.

_____

_____

Explain any misgivings you might have had before deciding to go with the most probably answer rather than waiting for total accuracy.

_____

_____

What trade-offs or consensus did you recognize in making your decision?

_____

_____

3. Identify the problem at work you would most like to resolve. Identify the barriers to resolving the problem. Write an action plan for overcoming those barriers.

Problem: _____

Action Plan: Overcoming the Constraints

_____

_____

Part Summary

In this Part, you learned the **benefits** of critical thinking and the **pitfalls** of noncritical thinking. You learned how to recognize and respond to **deceptive reasoning**. Next, you learned how to recognize and respond to **emotional manipulation**. You learned the **styles** and **traits** of both critical and noncritical thinking. Then, you learned **four strategies** for becoming a critical thinker.

Recognizing and Evaluating Arguments

"Fear not those who argue but those who dodge."

–Dale Carnegie

In this part:

- ▶ Define Arguments
- ▶ Step 1: Pinpoint Issues
- ▶ Step 2: Identify Arguments
- ▶ Step 3: Seek Clarity
- ▶ Step 4: Understand Context
- ▶ Step 5: Find Credibility
- ▶ Step 6: Look for Consistency
- ▶ Step 7: Judge Arguments
- ▶ Present Ideas Powerfully

Define Arguments

At work we often base decisions on arguments or explanations about a situation. In this book, we'll explore critical thinking through the framework of these two aspects of thinking—arguments and explanations.

First, we will look at the framework for recognizing and evaluating *arguments*. We are not using the word *argument* to mean having a nasty face-off with someone. Instead, we are looking at the framework critical thinkers use to *persuade* someone of a position. Explanations are covered in Part 3.

Issues and Answers

In the workplace, we grapple every day with numerous issues requiring us to evaluate statements, situations, and conflicts. Critical thinking gives us a process for evaluating and understanding these issues.

When faced with a statement, we can choose to agree or disagree with it. In determining our acceptance or rejection of a statement, we enter into critical thinking. We evaluate a statement and look at the evidence that supports it.

Certain statements are easier to evaluate than others, such as *"It's raining outside,"* or *"The network is down."*

The truth of other statements may be more difficult to determine. These statements are more a matter of opinion. These are about *issues* on which reasonable people might disagree.

Example

"People in sales are loners."

"We should change the strategic direction of the company."

The statements above each take a particular stand on an issue. These are called *conclusions*. A conclusion that is not agreed upon and is given supporting *evidence* for why it should be believed is called an *argument*.

Picture an Argument

In critical thinking terminology, an argument is an attempt to support a disputed conclusion through evidence.

Think about the connections between these terms by imagining an argument as a table. The tabletop is the position taken—the conclusion. The pieces of evidence are the legs supporting the tabletop. Someone else might not agree that it is the correct tabletop. The purpose of the argument is to give supportive evidence for using that particular tabletop.

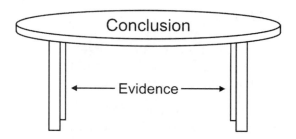

The Structure of an Argument

Example

Your co-worker makes the statement, "Boy, this company is really going down the tubes. Our stock has tanked. Our customers are leaving us. Our profits are down and morale is the lowest I've ever seen it."

This is an argument because it presents a conclusion with supporting evidence. The issue is the state of the company.

Step-by-Step Analysis

To become critical thinkers, we must learn to recognize issues to better understand what is at stake. Then we can delve into understanding and analyzing arguments.

Recognizing and evaluating arguments involves these steps:

Step 1: *Pinpoint Issues*

Step 2: *Identify Arguments*

Step 3: *Seek Clarity*

Step 4: *Understand Context*

Step 5: *Find Credibility*

Step 6: *Look for Consistency*

Step 7: *Judge Arguments*

Let's look at each step in depth.

"I admit it, I like to snorkel before analysing a business plan."

Step 1: Pinpoint Issues

People at work try to shape our beliefs and behaviors. If we are unaware of the underlying issues being presented, we may end up acting in ways we would not have if we had thought about the issues more deeply. Therefore, the first step in critical thinking is to figure out what the actual issue is.

Communication can often be confused and muddled, so identifying the issue can also help clarify a situation. Jack Kilby, the inventor of the microchip, has said, "A lot of solutions fail because they're trying to solve the wrong problem."

The first step to applying critical thinking to a topic is to ask: What is the real issue?

WHAT IS THE REAL ISSUE?

The issue is the topic under discussion. It is any matter of controversy or uncertainty. It is the focus, the main point, the problem, or the question in dispute. Identifying the issue means focusing on the central concept of the information being presented.

When trying to identify the issue, be neutral and objective. An issue is best stated in question format and in a way that can be answered either for or against the issue.

Let's go back to the statement that began this book. Bob approaches you and says in a very serious tone,

> *"If you put that conclusion in the report, you'll be looking for a new job by Monday! The boss never likes new ideas. Look what happened to Chris. He's out on the street now."*

What is the issue under discussion? (Remember to state the issue as a question, and format it in a way that can be answered either for or against the issue.)

_____

_____

_____

_____

Compare your responses with those of the author in the Appendix.

Steps to Pinpointing the Issue

1. Be neutral and objective.

2. State the issue in a question format that can be answered with yes or no.

3. Review your understanding of the issue with the information that has been presented to you.

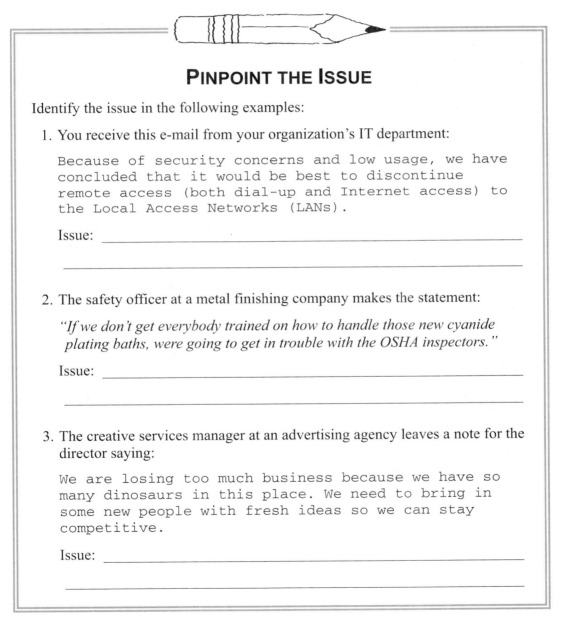

PINPOINT THE ISSUE

Identify the issue in the following examples:

1. You receive this e-mail from your organization's IT department:

   Because of security concerns and low usage, we have concluded that it would be best to discontinue remote access (both dial-up and Internet access) to the Local Access Networks (LANs).

   Issue: _____

   _____

2. The safety officer at a metal finishing company makes the statement:

   "If we don't get everybody trained on how to handle those new cyanide plating baths, were going to get in trouble with the OSHA inspectors."

   Issue: _____

   _____

3. The creative services manager at an advertising agency leaves a note for the director saying:

   We are losing too much business because we have so many dinosaurs in this place. We need to bring in some new people with fresh ideas so we can stay competitive.

   Issue: _____

   _____

Compare your responses with those of the author in the Appendix.

Pinpoint Discussion Issues

Sometimes people in a conversation are discussing two separate issues without even realizing it. One person is talking about apples and the other about oranges. This can lead to hurt feelings, confusion, and major mistakes. Sometimes one party might purposely confuse the issue to win support, or attempt to avoid an aspect of the issue to obscure it.

Example

Dennis, a product manager for a telecom company, has been pushing the developers for the promised upgrades to a product he supports. He sends an e-mail requesting a clear timetable for the delivery of the upgrade. A return e-mail from the developers' manager says,

```
The developers have a clear commitment to create the
best products possible. The response from our
customers has been outstanding. The high quality of
our products has been confirmed by our customers. We
want to work hand-in-hand with you to help you fully
support the products. We want to thank you for all
the good work you have performed in communicating the
effectiveness of the company products.
```

The manager seems to be focusing on the quality of the department's work rather than the specific request for a timetable for the delivery of the upgrade.

Read the case study on the following page and identify the issues present.

CASE STUDY: What Is the Issue?

Jeff is a salesman at an office supply company and Doris is his manager.

Jeff: *"Doris, I'm fed up with George in the production department. He's failed to stick to his production commitments and I'm left holding the bag. I don't want to deal with him anymore."*

Doris: *"Have you discussed the problem with him?"*

Jeff: *"Why should I coddle him? He knows he's blown it."*

Doris: *"Maybe you can find out where the holdup is over there and help solve the problem."*

Jeff: *"I've got my own job to do. I can't do his as well."*

Doris: *"I think it would be good if you met with George to discuss these difficulties."*

Jeff: *"Why are you siding with him rather than me?"*

Pinpoint the issues under discussion:

_____

_____

_____

_____

_____

_____

_____

Compare your responses with those of the author in the Appendix.

Keep the Issue in Focus

Staying focused on an issue during a discussion requires following three steps:

1. State the issue out loud.

2. Agree on the definition of the issue.

3. Refocus on the issue as needed.

In the case study on the previous page, what might Doris have said to stay on topic during the discussion?

Doris could have said, *"I think we are talking about two different issues. You are focused on convincing me that you shouldn't have to work with George. I'm focused on trying to solve the problem of the two of you not being able to work together. How about we take the broader perspective and look at how to solve the problem before we zero in on specific actions?"*

If there is disagreement, keep discussing until you have agreement about what issue you are going to talk about.

As you continue the discussion, keep focused on the issue. If the conversation moves away from the issue or gets muddled, bring everyone involved back to the agreed-upon issue or get agreement that you are focusing on a new issue.

Tip: *Regularly observe your own thinking to see if you are staying focused on the issue when you are arguing with yourself.*

Step 2: Identify Arguments

How do you make sense of what you hear and read? How can you understand the reasoning behind what's presented and look for the best, most reasonable answer? Most issues are presented with supporting evidence. After pinpointing the issue, you can begin to analyze the argument being presented.

In critical thinking, as in law, an argument is an attempt to support or prove a conclusion about an issue through evidence. Evidence consists of statements that provide support for the conclusion. Evidence communicates the *reasons* the presenter is for or against the issue.

When confronted with others' conclusions, you must decide if you want to make them your own conclusions. You cannot reach your own conclusions until you clarify the information presented to you.

To reach your own conclusions on an issue, identify the conclusions and evidence being presented.

Methods for Identifying Conclusions

▶ Look in likely locations—the beginning or end of a conversation or written documents.

▶ Look for word cues that introduce a conclusion, such as "thus," "consequently," "this shows that," "my point is," or "in short."

▶ If there is no clear statement within the body of what has been said or written, create a statement that answers the question "What is this about?" or "What is this person trying to prove?" or "What am I trying to prove?"

CASE STUDY: New Faces

Here is a letter from an employee, printed in a company newsletter:

```
It seems things have changed in the 20 years I've
worked here. Unlike what I felt during most of my
years here, today I feel a sense of discomfort when
I come to work. There are a lot of new young faces
around. I don't recognize most of them. They don't
seem to make the effort to introduce themselves.
All I hear is people thinking about how they can
advance their own careers, not help the company.
I'm not sure, but in my opinion this has hurt the
efficiency of the company. I'd be interested in
hearing what other people think about this.
```

What is the issue and the conclusion in this letter?

Issue:

_____

_____

_____

Conclusion:

_____

_____

_____

Compare your responses with those of the author in the Appendix.

Methods for Identifying Evidence

As we mentioned before, an argument is composed of a conclusion and evidence. We have learned how to locate the issue and the conclusion. The next step in understanding an argument is to locate the evidence being presented.

▶ Look for indicator cues that introduce statements of evidence:

  ▷ Since…

  ▷ For example…

  ▷ Is supported by…

  ▷ As shown by…

  ▷ As a result of…

  ▷ In view of…

  ▷ As indicated by…

  ▷ This is implied by…

▶ Ask the why question: "Why does that person say they take that position?"

Tip: *Be open to new reasons even if they do not fit your initial opinion.*

In the following case study, identify the *issue* and the *conclusion*, and then list the evidence given to support the *conclusion*.

CASE STUDY: Moving Toward the Internet

Acme, Inc. sells tools to garages and auto-supply stores. It recently started selling over the Internet. A senior manager wrote the following memo to the vice president for operations.

Our company's future is in Internet sales. More and more people are logging on and getting more at ease with performing tasks over the Internet.

We have been selling our products over the Internet for the past year and a half. During that time, Internet sales have increased 155% every six months. At the same time there has been a corresponding decrease in traditional sales of 15%. Our traditional sales methods carry an enormous overhead. Therefore, I believe we need to shift our strategic direction and weigh in much more heavily in support of the technical operations and marketing of Internet sales.

Identify the issues, conclusions, and evidence that support the conclusions.

Issue:

_____

_____

Conclusion:

_____

_____

Evidence:

_____

_____

_____

_____

Compare your responses with those of the author in the Appendix.

Step 3: Seek Clarity

Critical thinking includes assessing the value of evidence. Just looking at conclusions will not lead you to the truth. You must assess the strength of the reasoning behind the conclusion to determine if you should agree. This begins with discovering if you clearly understand what has been said or written.

You can't get to the core of the points made in an argument if words and phrases are confusing. This confusion must be addressed before you can understand the substance of an argument.

Address Ambiguities

When you look closely at the words or phrases of an argument, you might discover several types of ambiguities.

The meaning of the words in the statement can be unclear and vague.

> *"Lots of employees take office supplies home with them."*

How many employees does the word *lots* mean? Do a majority of employees steal office supplies and take them home or is it only three or four?

Words with unclear meaning should be clarified or avoided.

Words in a statement can have multiple meanings.

> *"There was a reaction in the lab that upset senior management."*

This could be a chemical reaction or a reaction by the employees of the lab.

> *"All the good workers in the company work late."*

What group of people are the "good workers"? Are they the best performers in the company or the workers who have the most positive values?

The word *late* is also vague because it is open to a wide range of interpretation. It could mean working until 5:30 P.M. instead of the standard 5 P.M. , or it could mean working until 10 P.M.

The meaning of words can be unclear within a particular context.

> *"We don't have the resources necessary to support that project."*

Resources could refer to tangibles such as people and equipment, or it could refer to financial support.

Sentence structure can lead to ambiguity.

> *"Wanted: man to sell cars on discount."*

Does the man work for a discount or are the cars at a discount?

Key Points:

▶ When you are able, follow up with the speaker or writer and ask her to clarify what she meant by a particular word or phrase. You can also ask for examples to better understand what she intended to say.

▶ Ambiguity that is not clarified weakens the argument. The greater the degree of ambiguity in an evidence statement, the less support it offers the conclusion.

REPHRASE FOR CLARITY

Identify the ambiguous words or phrases in the following statements, and explain how they are unclear. Rewrite the statements to make them clearer.

1. The effect of the cutbacks reverberated throughout the organization.

   Rewrite: _____

   _____

   _____

2. In an e-mail:

   ```
   I do not appreciate your weak acknowledgment.
   Please take it back.
   ```

   Rewrite: _____

   _____

   _____

3. Excessive time on the phone explains the lack of productivity.

   Rewrite: _____

   _____

   _____

Compare your responses with those of the author in the Appendix.

Step 4: Understand Context

Many issues are easier to identify, clarify, and evaluate when we know the context in which they occur.

For example, the normal way of working in your office reflects the personal philosophy of the chief executive officer. In another office, however, the norm might be completely different. Thus, *normal* is a valid descriptor only in the *context* of your particular office.

The context involves:

▶ The presenter's motive and purpose

▶ The place

▶ The circumstances around the issue

The Presenter's Motive and Purpose

Part of the context involves the motive behind a spoken or written statement. It helps to ask: What is the real purpose behind what was said?

▶ Is the person pushing a personal point of view?

▶ Does my buy-in to this person's reasoning advance a personal agenda?

▶ Does my agreement make him look good? Will it better his lot?

▶ Is she under stress? Does she want the issue to "go away"?

CASE STUDY: What's Behind the Statement?

You are a new executive assistant at a law firm. Cal Bartlett is another executive assistant who has taken it upon himself to teach you the ropes. He says, *"The most important thing you can do to get kudos from the boss is to regularly run the status reports on the computer."*

What are Cal Bartlett's possible motives and purposes?

_____

_____

_____

_____

Compare your responses with those of the author in the Appendix.

The Place

The location of a communication can give you more information about the evidence. Ask yourself a variety of questions to see if the place has any relevance to the statement. These questions might include:

▶ Were co-workers around who were meant to hear this?

▶ Was it a location where the person would feel defensive, weak, or insecure?

▶ Was it in a setting in which the speaker would feel comfortable or uncomfortable?

▶ Was this e-mail copied to anyone else?

▶ If it was verbal, who was in earshot?

▶ If it was written, who else would be reading it? Could it have been directed toward that other person?

THE PLACE

Let's say someone sends you the following e-mail:

> I hope the assistance I gave you on the Brookings account was helpful. Let me know if there is anything else I can do. I'm always here to help.

What are some relevant questions to ask about this e-mail?

_____

_____

_____

_____

_____

Compare your responses with those of the author in the Appendix.

Tip: *To assess the impact of place on an issue, picture the communication happening with a different audience to see if it would have played out the same way.*

The Circumstances

The surrounding circumstances can influence the meaning of a piece of evidence.

Ask yourself: Are there other relevant factors that would strengthen my support for the issue?

Example

> Robert sees you in the hall and says, *"This department has serious difficulties. The manager is inept. He has sullied our reputation among the other divisions. Everyone complains about the lack of communication. Customers are seriously thinking of going somewhere else."*

Upon investigation you discover that Robert had been asked to resign by his current manager. He had accepted a job with another company, and you did not know it at the time of the interaction.

Step 5: Find Credibility

Credibility is the believability of a statement or position. Credibility helps you determine if evidence is true or false, adequate or inadequate. To help you determine credibility, you can turn to your own experience or that of others.

Uncover Credible Evidence

When analyzing the credibility of an argument, ask three questions:

▶ Does the evidence conflict with my personal observations?

▶ Does the evidence conflict with my background knowledge?

▶ Is the source of the evidence credible?

Does the evidence conflict with my personal observations?

If some evidence conflicts with your own firsthand observation, its credibility should be in serious doubt. At the same time, you should be aware of the limits of your own observations. Sometimes your perception can be biased by a particular point of view. For example, if you really want something, it can influence you to perceive things in a way supportive of that event. Other times, circumstances can hinder effective observation, such as when you are trying to do two things at once.

Does the evidence conflict with my background knowledge?

Evidence can be compared to your own knowledge about the issue. The greater your knowledge on the subject, the weaker a conflicting piece of evidence should be seen. And obviously, the greater the conflict between the two, the less credible the evidence. At the same time, remember to keep an open mind to new information that may not fit with your own beliefs or understanding.

An example of an important place to assess credibility is the Internet. The Internet provides unfiltered information and thus can be the source of rumor, gossip, error, and deception, as well as useful information. It gives anyone the opportunity to publish anonymously in cyberspace material that could never before be accepted by the gatekeepers for reputable, established publishers.

Is the source of the evidence credible?

Often we might not be able to gather any additional information about an issue, so the credibility of the source is important because it is all we have to go on.

The more knowledgeable the source is about a given subject, the more reason there is to accept what the source has to say about it.

To help you determine the credibility of a source, ask the following questions:

- ▶ Did the source directly observe the situation or is the information simply hearsay?
- ▶ Are the events highly improbable?
- ▶ Is there supporting testimony?
- ▶ Is the source knowledgeable about the subject?

SHOULD THE COMPANY EXPAND?

You work at a pharmaceutical sales company and have received a report about expanding into a new region. The question is whether the company should open a new field office. The report gives a number of statements about why it would be good to jump into this region with a major capital investment. But some confusing evidence for the move calls into question the author's expertise.

How do you go about assessing the author's credibility?

_____

_____

_____

_____

_____

Let's assume that upon investigation you discover the following facts:

The author of the report would prefer to live in a town located in the new region. You discover that setting up field offices is not his area of expertise. He has had no experience setting up field offices and does not really know what is involved and the resources it would entail. He is the protégé of a senior executive who has been pushing for the move into this region for years.

How would you rate the overall credibility of this source?

_____

_____

_____

_____

_____

Tip: *Just because you have negative feelings about a person or you do not like a particular characteristic, it does not mean you should automatically discredit what that person has to say.*

Step 6: Look for Consistency

Another way to help evaluate the argument is to look for consistency. Check to see if any pieces of evidence contradict other evidence or the conclusion, or if the evidence is even relevant.

CONTRADICTORY EVIDENCE

We can compare different pieces of evidence to see if they are contradictory.

Example: You work as a loan processor in a mortgage finance company. You receive a report sent to the staff in your department from the closing department that has been disseminated to all of the staff in the loan department. It reads:

> Your department's lack of timeliness impacts our department's productivity. We spend a lot of our time waiting for the loan processors to finish their work. As everyone knows, we cannot do our job until the processors have done theirs. There are many demands on our staff beyond those given to us by the processors. We are completely helpless and at the whim of when the processors decide to complete their tasks. Given this situation, we plan to request that senior management set standards for more timely turnover of relevant documents.

Analyze the structure of the report above and point out any inconsistencies in the evidence. Outline the argument on a separate piece of paper, using the headings below.

Issue:

Conclusion:

Evidence:

Inconsistencies:

Compare your responses with those of the author in the Appendix.

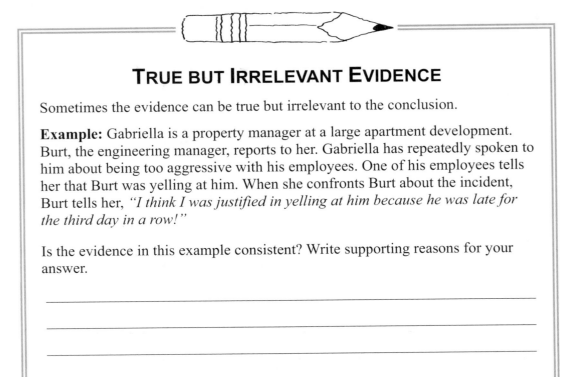

TRUE BUT IRRELEVANT EVIDENCE

Sometimes the evidence can be true but irrelevant to the conclusion.

Example: Gabriella is a property manager at a large apartment development. Burt, the engineering manager, reports to her. Gabriella has repeatedly spoken to him about being too aggressive with his employees. One of his employees tells her that Burt was yelling at him. When she confronts Burt about the incident, Burt tells her, *"I think I was justified in yelling at him because he was late for the third day in a row!"*

Is the evidence in this example consistent? Write supporting reasons for your answer.

_____

_____

_____

_____

_____

Compare your responses with those of the author in the Appendix.

Step 7: Judge Arguments

You now have the tools to avoid accepting arguments at face value. You can recognize the noncritical thinking tactics of deceptive reasoning and emotional manipulation and how to handle them. When you do, be assertive without becoming confrontational or hostile.

Assertive questioning means you do not passively accept nor do you aggressively attack. When you passively accept the ideas and reasons of another or assert a position that has randomly popped into your head, you are thinking noncritically. When you attack, you are practicing emotional manipulation.

The previous six steps provide a framework for recognizing and evaluating an argument. Once you have pinpointed the issue and identified conclusions and evidence, you can answer these five questions for judging an argument:

1. Is the evidence clear and unambiguous?

2. Does the context strengthen or weaken the evidence?

3. Is the evidence credible?

4. Are all the pieces of evidence consistent with one another?

5. Does the evidence support the conclusions?

In the following case study, see if you can identify the issue, the conclusion being presented, and the evidence supporting the conclusion. Then examine and evaluate the strength of the evidence and the overall strength of the argument.

CASE STUDY: Should You Accept the Proposal?

You are a member of the submissions division of a grant-giving foundation. The submissions division is responsible for collecting grant proposals.

You have been given the following proposal for an internal process improvement. It was produced by an internal task force that included two technology specialists, a records manager, an operations manager, and an HR specialist. The principal advocate for this initiative is the head of the technology department, who recently transferred from the accounting department.

```
The operations of the division need to be
streamlined and strengthened to improve the way
submissions from the public are handled. This is
important for both internal efficiency and the
satisfaction of our customers. There is a great
need to move toward solely electronic submissions.

Data storage is becoming cumbersome and expensive.
The current method of cataloging, handling, and so
on is inefficient and prone to error. No data would
be lost by dealing only with electronic
submissions. The Internet technology that would
facilitate electronic submission of the information
is now readily available to our entire customer
base. The electronic submissions would be properly
organized so they could be placed directly into our
database without requiring staff for data entry.
Our customers would get immediate acknowledgement
of the receipt of their submissions.

The system would quickly identify delinquent or
errant submissions. Our current databases are using
yesterday's technology, and this will give us the
opportunity to upgrade them to today's accepted
level.

The transition to such a program would take a
maximum of 12 months and would begin to save the
organization money within three months of full
operation.

It would reduce the current burden on staff so that
staff could begin to focus on other
responsibilities.
```

CONTINUED

Based on this scenario, write down your thoughts on the following:

Issue: _____

_____

Conclusion: _____

_____

Evidence: _____

_____

Analysis:

1. Is the evidence clear and unambiguous?

   _____

   _____

2. Does the context strengthen or weaken the evidence?

   _____

   _____

3. Is the evidence credible?

   _____

   _____

4. Are all the pieces of evidence consistent with one another?

   _____

   _____

5. Does the evidence support the conclusions?

   _____

   _____

Compare your responses with those of the author in the Appendix.

ARGUMENT ANALYSIS AT WORK

Select a complex argument from work like the preceding case study. Practice your critical thinking by going through this argument analysis form.

Issue: _____ _____

_____

Conclusion: _____

_____

Evidence: _____

_____

Analysis:

  1. Is the evidence clear and unambiguous?

     _____

     _____

  2. Does the context strengthen or weaken the evidence?

     _____

     _____

  3. Is the evidence credible?

     _____

     _____

  4. Are all the pieces of evidence consistent with one another?

     _____

     _____

  5. Does the evidence support the conclusions?

     _____

     _____

Present Ideas Powerfully

By learning how to recognize and evaluate arguments, you also have learned tools to help you *present* effective arguments. If you have a good grasp of the issue and you present clear, credible, and consistent evidence that validly supports your conclusion, you have the basis for a strong argument.

You must *present* your conclusions so they will stand up to critical analysis and be openly received.

Keys to Powerful Presentations

To present your ideas powerfully, by either speaking or writing, remember these key points:

▶ **Be prepared.** Being prepared means making the effort and time commitment for creating a good argument.

▶ **Have a clear idea of your position**. If you are not sure of your position, why should anyone else be swayed to it?

▶ **Have a clear intention of precisely what you want to accomplish.** Develop a clear goal for your presentation. What outcomes would you like to achieve?

▶ **Avoid ambiguities.** When people hear confusing or vague evidence, you lose your connection with them.

▶ **Stick to your issue**. The more complex the argument, the more difficult it is to stay focused on your issue. Remember to keep returning to your main point.

▶ **Know your audience.** The more you understand your audience, the more you can pitch your ideas in their language and direct your pitch toward their areas of concern.

▶ **Present a balanced point of view.** If you stridently push one perspective without discussing (and then challenging) opposing sides to the issue, you can polarize your audience against you.

▶ **Predict challenges and have prepared responses.** Think ahead about how a listener or reader might try to shoot down your idea. Prepare and practice responses for dealing with these challenges.

▶ **Seek feedback from others.** Bounce your ideas off a trusted colleague, if possible, to test your argument and refine your presentation.

Develop the body of your presentation by following these steps:

1. Spell out your argument.

2. Define key terms.

3. State your underlying assumption.

4. Group together your evidence for a given conclusion.

5. Proceed in an orderly direction: conclusion, main evidence, next evidence, conclusion.

6. Give examples.

7. Summarize at the end of a complete section and at the end of the entire presentation.

PRESENTATION CHECKLIST

Before your next written or oral presentation, run through the following checklist:

❑ How much time do I need to be effectively prepared? _____ minutes/hours/days

❑ My clearly spelled-out bottom-line position is:

_____

_____

_____

❑ What is the ideal outcome from this presentation?

_____

_____

_____

❑ What are the most important facts about my audience?

_____

_____

_____

❑ What are opposing viewpoints to my argument and how can they be challenged?

Viewpoint: _____

_____

Challenge: _____

_____

Viewpoint: _____

_____

Challenge: _____

_____

❑ Whom can I ask for feedback about my ideas before my written or oral presentation?

_____

Part Summary

In this Part, you learned to **define** the arguments that are the basis for decisions. Then, you learned to perform a **seven-step** analysis to evaluate the arguments that support a conclusion. These steps are:

1. **Pinpoint Issues**. Be objective, phrase the issue as a question, and review the information.

2. **Identify Arguments**. Look in likely locations, look for word cues, and create a statement

3. **Seek Clarity**. Address ambiguities, and follow up with the speaker or writer.

4. **Understand Context**. Know the motive, purpose, place, and circumstances.

5. **Find Credibility**. Check for conflicts with personal observation and knowledge, and evaluate the source's reliability.

6. **Look for Consistency**. Check for conflicting or irrelevant evidence.

7. **Judge Arguments**. Use the preceding six steps to evaluate the argument.

Finally, you learned how to **present** your ideas powerfully, so that they will stand up to analysis.

Developing and Evaluating Explanations

> " *I wish he would explain his explanation.* "
>
> —Lord Byron

In this part:

Explanations vs. Arguments

When we think critically, we take different approaches depending on whether we are trying to recognize and evaluate an *argument* or whether we are trying to develop or evaluate an *explanation*. But distinguishing between an argument and an explanation can be difficult.

While arguments attempt to persuade, explanations take the point of view of discovery and understanding. Thus, when people are trying to convince you to adopt their point of view, you use the framework for recognizing and evaluating an *argument*. When you are trying to comprehend something you do not understand or to evaluate someone else's explanation, you use the framework for developing and evaluating an *explanation*.

In an explanation, you are seeking understanding. You start with a question and then explore evidence that answers the question. With an explanation you are not trying to prove a conclusion. You are simply trying to find the best explanation possible.

An explanation can communicate what something is for or how to use something, define something, make something clear, or answer what caused something. We will be focusing particularly on explanations that help you to understand the *causes* of a situation.

What Is the Communicator's Intent?

Distinguishing between arguments and explanations can be confusing because some statements can appear to be both. The difference is in the context and the speaker's or writer's intent. If evidence is given to *support a conclusion*, it is an argument. If evidence is given to *answer a question*, it is an explanation. We must use good judgment to discern the difference.

Example

The question is:

"Why did the marketing effort fail?"

The explanation is:

"We both agree that the marketing effort has failed, and I think it is because the wrong customer base was targeted."

An argument about the above topic might be:

"I suggest that the marketing effort has failed. We can conclude this from the lack of response from customers."

These statements imply a lack of agreement that the marketing effort failed, and they *argue* that it has failed.

Sometimes explanations and arguments work together. An explanation can provide evidence in support of an argument. The main point is to determine the *intention* behind what is being presented. Is the intention to convince someone to adopt a point of view or is the intention to reach understanding about an agreed-upon question? This part explores the latter—developing and evaluating explanations.

EXPLANATION OR ARGUMENT?

For each of the following, put an **E** next to the statements you think might be explanations and an **A** next to the statements you think might be arguments.

_____ 1. We both agree that work has slowed down. I think the reorganization is the cause.

_____ I think we have less work in the department. It is shown by the fact that we are all taking longer breaks.

_____ 2. You asked why people like our Web site. I guess it's because of the great graphics.

_____ We get a lot of hits on our site. This demonstrates that it's a popular site.

_____ 3. This project may seem complicated but if you understand what is really wanted, it is easy. Therefore, it should not take as long as you think.

_____ I suppose the reason this project seems so complicated is because of all the different stakeholders involved in it.

_____ 4. Should I go to that meeting? Maybe I should skip it because that service call is more important.

_____ I missed the meeting so that I could make a service call.

_____ 5. It is clear to everyone that the client is very conservative. I think the reason is that he has been burned by risky investments in the past.

_____ In my opinion, the client is very conservative. He rarely makes a risky investment.

Compare your responses with those of the author in the Appendix.

Formulate Explanations

With a clearer understanding of the difference between arguments and explanations, you can learn how to develop explanations. As you now know, discerning the speaker's or writer's *intent* signals the difference. Explanations are not intended to convince; explanations seek to answer questions or evaluate answers to questions.

The four elements for developing an explanation are:

Element 1: Gather Information

Element 2: Process Information

Element 3: Develop Hypotheses

Element 4: Test Hypotheses

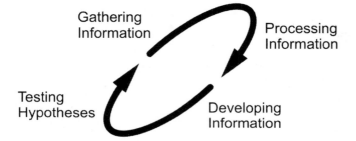

In actual practice, the different elements can occur simultaneously, but we will examine them one at a time.

Element 1: Gather Information

The first step to develop or evaluate an explanation is to gather as much information about the situation as possible.

There are four points to remember when gathering information:

1. Get as much detail as possible.

2. Pursue as many resources as possible.

3. Be alert to the type of information you look for.

    ▷ What you pay attention to will ultimately determine your explanation.

    ▷ Look for information that might not fit your initial hypothesis.

4. As you refine your hypothesis, continue to gather more information.

Sources of Information

Seek evidence for an explanation from a variety of sources, including:

▶ **Personal experience:** Your observations or those of others. When evaluating evidence, be careful to assess credibility as discussed in Part 2. In addition, watch out for hearsay and secondhand reports.

▶ **Documents:** Statistical information, reports, and other writings.

▶ **Artifacts:** Any relevant physical materials such as office equipment, products, software, or other manufactured goods.

CASE STUDY: Phillipe and the Delivery Slowdown

Phillipe works for a large furniture manufacturer. He leads a team that fulfills orders that come in over the Internet. For some reason, the time to delivery has increased by 20%. Phillipe is worried and would like to find an explanation for the slowdown.

If Phillipe were a noncritical thinker, he would just latch onto the easiest explanation. He might think, "Allison has been out sick for two weeks. That must be the problem. I just have to wait until she gets back."

If he were to go through the steps for gathering information, however, he would work harder to discover all the facts. Phillipe would observe each step of the process to get more personal experience and he would ask questions of co-workers to understand their experiences with order fulfillment.

He would gather relevant documents, such as a report on the number of orders compared to previous time periods. He would study the Web site (an artifact) to determine if any glitches exist. Phillipe would avoid making any initial limiting assumptions so he could find as many avenues as possible for information.

Element 2: Process Information

Processing information involves taking action with it. You manipulate it, grapple with it, and reflect upon it.

Follow these steps to help you process information:

1. Take as much time as possible to reflect on the information.

2. Compare and contrast different pieces of information.

3. Look for patterns or unifying principles.

4. Experiment with placing the information into different headings.

Generalizing Information

As you manipulate, grapple with, and reflect upon information you gather, it is common to form generalizations. You make a generalization when you derive a general concept from specific items. You infer that some characteristic from that specific item holds for the larger group.

Example

Steve, a computer salesman, is interested in breaking into a new market. He noticed his company does not do business with associations. Steve wonders why. He wants to know: Why doesn't the company have any association business?

So he goes to meet a prospective customer, the operations manager at a large association. As Steve walks through the building to a conference room, he notices that the office staff are using very old computers. He also notices that all the staff are dressed in conservative business attire. The operations manager greets Steve in a reserved and formal manner. The conversation is cordial, but as it continues, the prospects for a large sale do not seem promising.

Later in the week, Steve visits another director of operations at another association. He notices a very similar, conservative environment and receives a similar response. Steve continues researching his question and talks to several other salespeople who have had similar experiences.

Steve makes the generalization that large associations tend to be financially conservative and lack the commitment to large-scale computer investments. This generalization forms the foundation of a concept or mental model Steve now has about associations.

Such a generalization about associations might be helpful to Steve as he tries to break into another market. But it could also lead him astray because he has made the generalization from limited experience and research. Forming a mental model from too small a sample is called *overgeneralization*, a common error when a person is processing information.

Information Processing Errors

As you observed in the previous example, looking for patterns and groupings in the information you gather is an important part of processing information. But it can lead to errors in reasoning, including these common pitfalls:

▶ Stereotyping

▶ Self-delusion

▶ Attribution error

▶ Excessive focus on the conspicuous

As you learn about each pitfall and read the examples, consider a time you might have made a similar error in processing information at work.

Stereotyping

When your initial mental model is incorrect, biased, or incomplete, you may develop a stereotype. Whatever impression you have of the initial group gets assigned to the entire group and becomes the explanation.

Example: People who work with numbers have poor interpersonal skills.

Self-delusion

When your personal biases flavor your perceptions, you may become deluded in your thinking.

Example: Steve, the computer salesman, has not made a sale in weeks. He visits a long-term customer who implies that he is not interested in purchasing at this time. Steve's desperation deludes him into misinterpreting the customer's signals as an invitation to pursue the sale, and he becomes overly pushy, potentially harming his relationship with the client.

Attribution Error

When you explain other people's behavior as being based on internal variables—personality qualities, habits—rather than outside situational variables, you are making an error in attribution.

Example: When a phone call is not returned promptly, you think it is because the other person is rude, rather than thinking perhaps the person never received the message or is simply overloaded with work.

Or if co-workers oppose one of your ideas in a meeting, you may attribute the opposition to their internal characteristics, such as stubbornness or irrationality, rather than the possibility that the idea would not work.

Excessive Focus on the Conspicuous

When you focus more than is appropriate on particularly vivid or memorable data.

Example: A workgroup of 18 employees has two aggressive complainers. When the workgroup's main project is late, after the original project plan was altered, you explain it by saying that you have a lot of resistant employees with bad attitudes.

"It's not easy being the guy who shouts, 'The strategic plan has no clothes'."

Element 3: Develop Hypotheses

The purpose of an explanation is to provide a well-reasoned answer to a question about why something is so—what caused it. As we gather and process information, we begin to develop answers to the question at hand by making a speculation—a hypothesis—to guide our questioning. When we think we have a possible answer, we research it further.

A hypothesis is a tentative statement that proposes a possible explanation to some phenomenon or event. It is a *provisional* explanation for why something occurred.

To develop a hypothesis, you look at different possible categories and the qualities associated with them and see which ones best fit the facts you have about the topic. Then you seek more facts as you pursue the best possible hypothesis. Your goal is to develop a hypothesis that accounts for as much of the relevant facts as possible.

Generate Alternatives

When we develop hypotheses, it is easy to accept the first one we think of. But the first idea is not necessarily the best. Often, several interpretations are possible. Expanding our investigation to look at alternatives gives us a richer field from which to draw a good hypothesis.

We can get caught up in thinking there are only two alternatives—a solution is either black or white. Most situations are not so limited. Often many alternatives exist.

Phillipe's Delivery Slowdown Hypotheses

In an earlier example, Phillipe at the furniture company comprehensively gathered information about why his team was slower at fulfilling Internet orders.

His initial explanation was that the slowdown was from the two-week absence of one of his workers. Being a critical thinker, however, Phillipe began to process the information by comparing and contrasting pieces of information to find patterns. As he did this he formed several hypotheses for why order fulfillment was 20% slower:

- ▶ Even though there was a temporary replacement, Allison's two-week absence and the replacement's lack of experience created a hole in the process that slowed everything down.

- ▶ The new Web site request form was poorly written, so it solicited confusing requests from customers, which slowed down the order-fulfillment rate.

- ▶ Because it was summertime, people performed more slowly than at other times of the year.

- ▶ Inventory was low, creating a backup of orders.

Phillipe developed these alternative hypotheses as he gathered and processed relevant information.

HYPOTHESIZE AT WORK

Think of the most difficult challenge coming up for you at work. Develop a hypothesis of why this is going to occur. Do not go with the easiest explanation. Generate at least four possible alternatives.

Upcoming Challenge

_____

_____

_____

_____

Alternative Hypotheses

1. _____

_____

_____

2. _____

_____

_____

3. _____

_____

_____

4. _____

_____

_____

Element 4: Test Hypotheses

Once you develop a hypothesis, you can test it to see if it is consistent with all the evidence. At the same time, look for evidence that might invalidate the hypothesis.

Comparing and Evaluating Hypotheses

In addition to testing your hypothesis, you also should seek to discover if some alternative hypothesis fits the evidence better. Find out which one has the least number of assumptions associated with it.

As you process the information and grapple with possible explanations, you refine and modify the initial hypothesis. Thus, the shape of the hypothesis is adjusted as more facts and understandings come to light.

Ultimately, a good hypothesis:

▶ Appears believable

▶ Explains all the relevant facts

▶ Is better than alternative explanations in giving clear reasons for the situation (because the alternatives do not fit the facts as well)

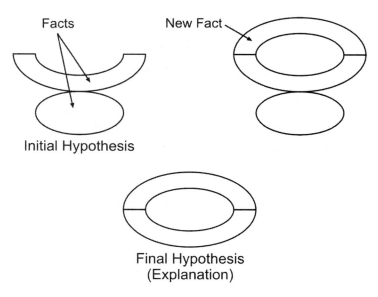

The Testing of a Hypothesis

Ask Discovery Questions

Giving thought to explanations is a process of discovery. The best way to develop explanations is to ask questions. Assertive questions push us beyond the initial statement to better understand the strength of an explanation.

Here are some assertive questions you can ask at each stage in the development of an explanation.

1. **Gather Information**

   ▷ What do I know about this situation?

   ▷ What kind of information do I need?

   ▷ What information is most important?

2. **Process Information**

   ▷ Have I dealt with this kind of situation before? How did I solve it before?

   ▷ How can I categorize this information?

   ▷ What are the patterns?

3. **Develop Hypotheses**

   ▷ What is my hypothesis?

   ▷ What are the alternatives in this situation?

   ▷ What alternative makes the most sense?

4. **Test Hypotheses**

   ▷ Is the hypothesis believable?

   ▷ Does any information not fit into the hypothesis?

   ▷ Is this the simplest explanation for the situation?

   ▷ Is this hypothesis better than any other possible hypothesis?

DEVELOP AN EXPLANATION AT WORK

Pick an aspect of your work that you want to be able to explain. Go through these discovery questions from the previous page to help you form your explanation.

1. Gather Information

What do I know about this situation?

_____

_____

What kind of information do I need?

_____

_____

What information is most important?

_____

_____

2. Process Information

Have I dealt with this kind of situation before? How did I solve it before?

_____

_____

How can I categorize this information?

_____

_____

What are the patterns?

_____

_____

CONTINUED

3. Develop Hypotheses

What is my hypothesis?

_____

_____

What are the alternatives in this situation?

_____

_____

What alternative makes the most sense?

_____

_____

4. Test Hypotheses

Is the hypothesis believable?

_____

_____

Does any information not fit into the hypothesis?

_____

_____

Is this the simplest explanation for the situation?

_____

_____

Is this hypothesis better than any other possible hypothesis?

_____

_____

Challenge Assumptions

To develop the strongest and most accurate explanations possible, we must become aware of biases and unspoken assumptions that might cloud our reasoning. Such beliefs grow out of the explanations we develop about how the world works.

Assumptions are beliefs that are presumed. They are usually unstated beliefs that support expressed reasoning.

We are constantly using assumptions. They help us make decisions.

"I assume I have a job when I go in to work."

But there is a balance. Assumptions are often taken for granted even though they can greatly influence the conclusion. So it helps to be aware of the assumptions operating and to evaluate them to ferret out biases or erroneous beliefs.

Phillipe's Assumptions

As Phillipe tries to explain his order fulfillment slowdown at the furniture company, he seems to be making the following initial assumptions:

▶ A 20% slowdown is unusual for his business process.

▶ A 20% slowdown is a problem that needs to be addressed.

▶ Phillipe has the ability to figure out an explanation for the slowdown.

These are reasonable assumptions for Phillipe, which shows that making assumptions helps to direct attempts to reach explanations.

But if Phillipe were new to his job and unaware that a 20% slowdown is a common fluctuation for order fulfillment, then he would be operating under an erroneous assumption. He could discover this error as he gathered and processed information on his way to formulating an explanation.

PHILLIPE: IDENTIFY THE ASSUMPTIONS

See if you can recognize the assumptions Phillipe made in each hypotheses:

1. Despite the efforts of the inexperienced temp, Allison's two-week absence created a hole in the process that slowed everything down.

   Underlying assumptions:

   _____

   _____

   _____

2. The new Web site request form was poorly written and it solicited confusing requests from customers, which slowed down the order-fulfillment rate.

   Underlying assumptions:

   _____

   _____

   _____

3. Because it was summertime, people performed more slowly than at other times of the year.

   Underlying assumptions:

   _____

   _____

   _____

4. Inventory was low, creating a backup of orders.

   Underlying assumptions:

   _____

   _____

   _____

Compare your answers to those of the author in the Appendix.

Part Summary

In this Part, you learned the **difference** between explanations and arguments. Next, you learned how to **develop explanations** by using the four elements:

1. **Gather Information**
2. **Process Information**
3. **Develop Hypotheses**
4. **Test Hypotheses**

Then, you learned to ask **discovery questions** to help develop explanations. Finally, you learned to overcome bias and **challenge assumptions**.

A P P E N D I X

Reviewing What You've Learned

Critical thinking is a way of life. In Part 1 you explored the attitudes and strategies for becoming a critical thinker. Parts 2 and 3 gave you two frameworks to apply to statements and decisions you face. These frameworks are:

The Steps for Recognizing and Evaluating Arguments

Step 1: Pinpointing Issues

Step 2: Identifying Arguments

Step 3: Seeking Clarity

Step 4: Understanding Context

Step 5: Finding Credibility

Step 6: Looking for Consistency

Step 7: Judging Arguments

The Elements for Developing and Evaluating Explanations

Element 1: Gathering Information

Element 2: Processing Information

Element 3: Developing Hypotheses

Element 4: Testing Hypotheses

Take the time to think about your intentions and the intentions of those around you when you are grappling with a problem.

Are you trying to convince someone about your point of view? Are co-workers trying to convince you about their opinions? If so, apply the steps for developing and evaluating arguments.

Do you want to understand and explain a situation? If so, apply the steps for developing and evaluating explanations.

As you become more and more familiar with these two frameworks, the skills will become more refined and automatic, and you will find yourself living fully as a critical thinker.

PERSONAL ACTION PLAN

Which critical thinking style do I most want to develop in myself?

_____

Which strategies will I practice to improve my critical thinking skills?

_____

_____

I will practice the seven steps for recognizing and evaluating arguments in the following ways:

_____

_____

_____

_____

_____

I will practice the four steps to developing and evaluating explanations in the following ways:

_____

_____

_____

_____

_____

_____

Appendix to Part 1

Comments & Suggested Responses

Noncritical Styles in Action

1. Zack is demonstrating the noncritical thinking style of "the Snob" by arrogantly discounting Juanita's skills.

2. Holly shows signs of using the noncritical thinking style of "the Leech." She accepted uncritically whatever was being said to her without making the effort to form her own views.

3. The senior executive is using the noncritical thinking style of "the Dilettante." He is being overly receptive and giving vague reasons for an inadequately evaluated line of action that may well cause great difficulties in the future.

Critical Thinking Style File

1. Alexa is demonstrating the critical thinking styles of the Navigator and the Warrior. She is looking ahead to choose the best path and is courageous in speaking up and not going along with the team leader.

2. Pascal is showing the critical thinking styles of the Student and the Detective. He wants to get more information and to inquire further about the basis for the recommendations before jumping into them.

3. Steven is using the critical thinking styles of the Explorer and the Detective. He is going to proactively seek the truth and ask relevant questions.

4. Hans is showing the critical thinking styles of the Explorer and the Warrior. He is curious in looking for the truth and is willing to jump in and tackle a potentially difficult situation.

Appendix to Part 2

Comments & Suggested Responses

What Is the Real Issue?

Objectively stated, the issue is: *Should that particular conclusion be kept in the report?*

Note that the issue is stated in a nonjudgmental way that can be answered affirmatively or negatively.

Pinpoint the Issue

1. The issue is: *Should we remove the remote access to the LANs?*

2. The issue is: *Do our employees need safety training?*

3. The issue is: *Do we need to restaff?*

Case Study: What Is the Issue?

Issue

From Jeff's point of view, the issue is: *Should I continue to work with George?* From Doris' perspective, the issue is: *What can be done to solve the problem?*

Conclusion

Neither Jeff nor Doris sought to clarify the issue under discussion. This misunderstanding may lead to unnecessary tension.

Case Study: New Faces

The issue could be stated: *"Has a change in the level of friendliness among employees affected the company's productivity?"*

The conclusion presented by the letter writer could be stated: *"A decrease in friendliness between staff is hurting the company's efficiency."*

Case Study: Moving Toward the Internet

Issue

The issue can be stated as "Should the company shift its strategic direction and capital investment to place a greater focus on Internet sales?"

Conclusion

The conclusion could be stated as "Acme, Inc. should shift its strategic direction and capital investment to focus more heavily on Internet sales."

Evidence

- ▶ A greater number of people are getting on the Internet and becoming more comfortable using it to do business.

- ▶ Acme's Internet sales have dramatically increased.

- ▶ Acme's traditional sales have decreased.

- ▶ The traditional methods are more expensive to operate than the Internet services.

Review

Once you have pinpointed the issue and identified the argument, then you can decide if the issue is important enough for you to spend the time to analyze the argument.

If the issue is one you want to explore further, then you must evaluate the evidence and analyze how the components of the argument fit together.

Rephrase for Clarity

1. Many employees expressed insecurity about their jobs after the cutbacks, and this negatively affected performance.

2. You mentioned my name only in passing, which implied I was only peripherally involved on the project. Please correct this by acknowledging my integral involvement.

3. Employees spending an excessive amount of time on the phone on personal business have hindered the department's overall productivity.

Case Study: What's Behind the Statement?

There are several possible motives and purposes.

1. Bartlett is a nice guy and likes to help people.

2. Bartlett hates doing the status reports and has been pressured by his supervisor for months to get the status reports done and would love to hand them over to you.

3. Bartlett's enthusiasm is misplaced, and he is unknowingly giving you erroneous information.

To assess the speaker's motive and purpose:

▶ Do not respond immediately.

▶ Research the statements of the person.

▶ Ask questions about the speaker's relationships within the office.

Responding to the case study:

▶ Before taking on the status reports, talk to your manager and ask if this is really part of your responsibility.

▶ Ask Bartlett for more specific details.

▶ Ask other colleagues about Bartlett.

The Place

Was the e-mail copied to someone else, such as the manager?

Was there a reason the person e-mailed you rather than just telling you face-to-face?

Contradictory Evidence

Issue

Should the time standards for document turnover be tightened?

Conclusion

Yes, there should be tighter time standards for the loan processing department.

Evidence

1. The loan processors' lack of timeliness impacts the closing department's productivity.

    a. The closing staff cannot do its work until the documents come from the processors.

    b. The closing staff spends a lot of its time waiting for finished documents from the loan processors.

2. The closing staff has many different demands on it beyond the work from the processors.

3. The closing staff is completely helpless and at the whim of the processors.

Inconsistencies

Evidence #2 is inconsistent with evidence #1a. If there are other demands beyond the work from the processors, the closing staff could be working on those demands, or at least on work other than that requiring the documents from the loan department. Evidence #2 also conflicts with #3 because if the staff could be engaged in other work, it would not be completely helpless and at the whim of the processors.

This inconsistency suggests that tightening the time standards for document turnover may not really be what is needed to fix this problem.

True but Irrelevant Evidence

The evidence the engineering manager cited is probably true. The employee probably was late three mornings in a row. But the truth of the evidence in this case is irrelevant to the inappropriate aggression demonstrated by the engineering manager and thus is inconsistent with the argument.

Case Study: Should You Accept the Proposal?

Issue

Should the submissions division move toward solely using electronic submissions?

Conclusion

Yes, the submissions division should move toward solely using electronic submissions.

Evidence

1. Data storage is becoming cumbersome and expensive.

2. The current method of cataloging, handling, and so on is inefficient and prone to error.

3. No data would be lost using only electronic submissions.

4. The Internet technology that would facilitate electronic submissions is readily available to the entire customer base.

5. The electronic submissions would be properly organized so they could be placed directly into the database without requiring staff for data entry.

6. Customers would get immediate acknowledgment of the receipt of their submissions.

7. The system would quickly identify delinquent or errant submissions.

8. The initiative will provide the opportunity to modernize out-of-date databases.

9. The burden on the staff would be reduced so they could focus on other responsibilities.

Analysis

1. Is the evidence clear and unambiguous?

    Evidence #4 states that the necessary Internet technology is "readily available" to the entire customer base. What exactly is meant by "readily available"? Is it available but costly? Is it available only to high-tech companies?

    Evidence #8 mentions the initiative providing the opportunity to "modernize" out-of-date databases. What does "modernize" mean for specific time and resource commitment? How much of an extra expense will this create?

2. Does the context strengthen or weaken the evidence?

   You have to wonder if the head of the information technology department, who is championing this initiative, has some hidden motives that bias the decision to push for it.

3. Is the evidence credible?

   As a member of the submissions department, you may have specific knowledge that would make you suspicious of some of the evidence about the current methods' inefficiency and the ease of transitioning to a new methodology. Knowing the complexity of the task, you may question the implication that there would be less of a burden on the staff. And the task force may have been lacking in the expertise needed to understand the submissions division. Was the task force accurately informed?

4. Are all the pieces of evidence consistent with each other?

   The different pieces of evidence are fairly consistent with each other.

5. Does the evidence support the conclusions?

   If all of the pieces of evidence were strong, they would support the conclusions. After the analysis, however, a number of serious questions need to be answered before you should accept the argument.

Appendix to Part 3

Comments & Suggested Responses

Explanation or Argument?

1. *"We both agree that work has slowed down. I think it has been happening because of the reorganization."*

   E. This is probably an explanation. The parties appear to agree about the topic in question. The question is "Why has work slowed down?" and the answer is "Because of the reorganization."

   "I think we have less work in the department. It is shown by the fact that we are all taking longer breaks."

   A. This appears to be an argument because the speaker seems to be trying to prove that the conclusion, "We have less work in the department," is being supported by the evidence, "We are all taking longer breaks."

2. *"You asked why people like to visit our Web site? I guess it is because of the great graphics."*

   E. This is an explanation because there is an attempt to understand the question "Why do people like to visit our Web site?" The answer is "Because of the great graphics."

   "We have had a huge number of hits on our Web site. This demonstrates that we have a popular Web site."

   A. Here the speaker is trying to prove that his conclusion, "We have a popular Web site," is supported by the evidence of the huge number of hits.

3. *"This project may seem complicated, but if you understand what is really wanted, it is easy. Therefore, it should not take as long as you think."*

   A. This is an argument because the speaker is trying to convince the listener that the project is easier and should not take as long as thought.

   "I suppose the reason this project seems so complicated is because of all the different types of stakeholders involved."

   E. This appears to be an explanation: The question "Why does this project seem so complicated?" is answered by "There are many different types of stakeholders involved."

4. *"I wonder if I should go to that meeting. No, I should skip it because making that service call is more important."*

A. This person is arguing with herself over attending the meeting. She makes the argument that she should skip the meeting.

"I missed the meeting so that I could make a service call."

E. This appears to be an explanation in which the unspoken question is "Why did you miss the meeting?" The answer is "To make a service call."

5. *"It is clear to everyone that the client is very conservative. I think the reason is that he has been burned by risky investments in the past."*

E. Everyone agrees the client is very conservative. The unspoken question in this explanation is "Why?" The explanation given is "He has been burned by risky investments in the past."

"In my opinion, the client is very conservative because he rarely makes a risky investment."

A. This seems to be an argument rather than an explanation. The opinion, "The client is very conservative," is supported by the evidence, "He rarely makes a risky investment."

Phillipe: Identify the Assumptions

1. Underlying assumptions:
   ▷ The replacement works at a slower pace than Allison does.
   ▷ Experience is needed for the replacement to work as fast as Allison.

2. Underlying assumptions:
   ▷ Confusing requests would slow down the order-fulfillment rate.

3. Underlying assumptions:
   ▷ Fluctuating performance is bad.
   ▷ Performance fluctuates with different seasons.

4. Underlying assumptions:
   ▷ A backup of orders automatically means the order-fulfillment rate would be slower.

These underlying assumptions may be true or not. Being aware of them, though, can lead you to seek out new data to assess the truth of each assumption. By challenging your underlying assumptions, you refine and improve your ability to evaluate an explanation.

Additional Reading

Crisp 50-Minute Series books:

Gellatt, H. B. *Creative Decision Making.*

Kindler, Herb. *Clear and Creative Thinking.*

Nothstine, William L. *Influencing Others.*

Zuker, Elaina. *Influence.*

Other related reading:

Bono, Edward de. *de Bono's Thinking Course.* New York: Facts on File, Inc., 1994.

Capaldi, Nicholas. *The Art of Deception.* Amherst, NY: Prometheus Books, 1987.

Chaffee, John. *The Thinker's Way.* Boston: Little, Brown & Co., 1998.

Diestler, Sherry. *Becoming a Critical Thinker: A User Friendly Manual.* Upper Saddle River, NJ: Prentice Hall, 1998.

Ennis, Robert H. *Critical Thinking.* Upper Saddle River, NJ: Prentice Hall, 1996.

Gilovich, Thomas. *How We Know What Isn't So: The Fallibility of Human Reason in Everyday Life.* New York: The Free Press, 1991.

Hoaglund, John. *Critical Thinking.* Newport News, VA: Vale Press, 1999.